EARTH BEFORE US

AMULET BOOKS
NEW YORK

EARTH BEFORE US

DINOSAUR EMPIRE!

By **ABBY HOWARD**

ACKNOWLEDGMENTS

Thank you to Scott Hartman, Darren Naish, and Mark Witton for providing up-to-date information and resources for anyone and everyone.

Thanks to Professor Hans Larsson and the Redpath Museum.

DEDICATED TO ALL THE MUSEUMS
IN WHICH I HAVE CRIED

The Library of Congress has cataloged the hardcover edition as follows:
Names: Howard, Abby (Comic artist), author, illustrator.
Title: Earth before us / by Abby Howard.
Description: New York : Amulet Books, 2017. | Summary: Ms. Lernin, a retired paleontologist, helps fifth-grader Ronnie study for a quiz on dinosaurs by taking her on a guided tour of the Mesozoic Era.
Identifiers: LCCN 2016056055 | ISBN 9781419723063 (hardback)
Subjects: LCSH: Graphic novels. | CYAC: Graphic novels. | Dinosaurs--Fiction.
| Time travel--Fiction. | BISAC: JUVENILE NONFICTION / Comics & Graphic Novels / History. | JUVENILE NONFICTION / Animals / Dinosaurs & Prehistoric Creatures.
Classification: LCC PZ7.7.H73 Ear 2017 | DDC 741.5/973--dc23

Paperback ISBN 978-1-4197-3622-3

Printed and bound in China
10 9 8 7 6 5 4 3 2 1

ABRAMS The Art of Books
195 Broadway, New York, NY 10007
abramsbooks.com

THE EARTH BEFORE US SERIES

Dinosaur Empire!
Journey through the Mesozoic Era

Ocean Renegades!
Journey through the Paleozoic Era

Mammal Takeover!
Journey through the Cenozoic Era

8

And lo and behold, several million years later, they're a whole new species!

~~STRIPE HORSE~~ ZEBRAS!

There are some interesting trends in evolution, like **convergent evolution**.

Which is what it's called when unrelated animals have features in common, or look a lot like each other.

HEDGEHOG   ECHIDNA
↳ NOT RELATED ↵

Dolphins and sharks, for example, look very much alike, and it can be hard to tell them apart sometimes,

even though one is a mammal and one is a fish!

They look similar because they both live in the same niche.

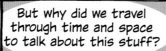
They are both large ocean predators, and this body shape makes them faster, and therefore better at catching prey.

Many large ocean predators have a shape like this!

COMMON DOLPHIN   TUNA
ORCA
BOTTLENOSE DOLPHIN
TIGER SHARK
SWORDFISH
PADDLEFISH
BULLSHARK   BELUGA

Okay, this is all useful stuff to know for passing my quiz or whatever.

But why did we travel through time and space to talk about this stuff?

Couldn't you have told me all this in your living room?

Because this is where I keep my whiteboard, of course.

Plus, this is just the first stop on our journey!

Knowing about how evolution works will make it easier to understand the creatures we're about to meet: where they came from, why they look the way they do, and where they went.

Creatures? Are we going to a zoo or something?

Yes.   "Or something."

Dinosaurs shared the earth with all kinds of other creatures.

Like these herbivorous aetosaurs (EAT-oh-sawrs), which are *related* to dinosaurs, but are *not dinosaurs*.

But their legs are right under their bodies. Isn't that a dinosaur trait?

We mammals also have our legs right under our bodies, but we aren't dinosaurs!

DINOSAUR   AETOSAUR

The same trait can evolve in totally unrelated species. These aetosaurs evolved their upright stance independently of the dinosaurs, and the anatomy is a little different.

Aetosaurs are distinct in a lot of ways. They're covered in thick plates of bone that protect them from predators

and use their shovel-like noses to dig up tasty plants.

There are also some cool carnivorous non-dinosaurs, like Postosuchus (POST-oh-SOOK-uss).

It's the biggest, baddest predator of its region. It even hunts Coelophysis!

Though there are more carnivores lurking in the rivers . . .

Oh! That's a crocodile, right?

REDONDOSAURUS (REE-DON-DO-SAWR-uss)

They do look a lot like crocodiles, but this is a case of convergent evolution!

These are phytosaurs (FITE-oh-sawrs), which aren't crocodiles, but live in the same niche as crocodiles.

The main difference between them is that phytosaurs have nostrils on a hump in front of their eyes,

The river-dwelling large-predator niche.

MYSTRIOSUCHUS (MISS-TREE-OH-SOOK-uss)

and crocodiles have theirs at the end of their snouts, like a dog.

The Triassic creature most closely related to modern crocodiles is actually this little guy, Terrestrisuchus (tur-RES-tree-SOOK-uss).

Well, that's just silly. This looks *nothing* like a crocodile.

Give it a few million years. You'll see.

25

Holy CRUD! What is THIS?

This is Smok wawelski (SMOK wah-WELL-skee), a carnivore that roams the same forests as Liliensternus, and we don't really know what it is.

We **paleontologists** (PAY-lee-on-TOL-oh-jists), the people who study fossils, are still trying to figure out which group it belongs to, since it shares traits with several.

It could be related to Postosuchus, or it could be closer to crocodylomorphs, like Terrestrisuchus and our modern crocodiles.

Or it could be totally unrelated to all the other archosaurs, in a new unnamed group all on its own.

It could also be an early dinosaur, in which case it would have protofeathers!

Wait, what's an ARK-oh-sawr?

It's the group name for basically all the creatures we just met, including dinosaurs! They all evolved from a common ancestor and have traits in common, though they are pretty distinct from one another.

There were a lot of niches left empty at the beginning of the Triassic, and when there's an empty niche, animals evolve to fill it.

I know what these are. They're flying dinosaurs!

Actually, these aren't dinosaurs at all. They're pterosaurs (TERR-oh-sawrs), warm-blooded flying reptiles that are pretty closely related to dinosaurs.

But they *aren't* dinosaurs!

CAVIRAMUS
(CAY-VEE-RAY-MUSS)

EUDIMORPHODON
(YOU-DYE-MORF-OH-DON)

Pterosaurs weren't the first **vertebrates** (animals with spines) to take to the skies.

ICAROSAURUS
(IK-AR-OH-SAWR-USS)

But the others weren't...

SHAROVIPTERYX
(SHARE-OH-VIP-TER-IKS)

...very practical.

Pterosaurs have different wings than birds or bats, though they still have the same arm bones as any land vertebrate.

NOT TO SCALE

FINGERS

WRIST BONES

ULNA

RADIUS

HUMERUS

We have the same bones in our arms as they do!

These guys are fluffy, too. Is this the same fluff that dinosaurs have?

Nope, this fluff is called pycnofibers (PIK-no-FIBE-ers), which are slightly different than feathers or fur.

But some paleontologists think pycnofibers could have evolved from protofeathers, and that the ancestor of both dinosaurs *and* pterosaurs was fluffy!

It seems like there's a lot that paleontologists are still trying to figure out.

Yes, it's a very exciting field of study!

Each new fossil gives more tiny clues to the mysteries of the past.

WOWZA

Such as the mystery of how pterosaurs hunted. We're pretty sure they eat by grabbing any fish unlucky enough to be close to the surface.

Though it isn't much luckier for the fish to be deep underwater...

What is that large ominous shape in the water?

Some kinda whale?

Let's go find out!

What?

AAAAAAAH

...great-great-great-grandparents, the first mammals!

Mammals are warm-blooded vertebrates that have fur and make milk to feed their young.

I didn't know dinosaurs and mammals lived at the same time!

A lot of people think mammals evolved after the dinosaurs died out, but mammals were around all throughout the Mesozoic.

In our time, mammals are widespread and diverse. You and I are mammals, and so are cats and dogs and elephants and sea lions, to name just a few.

But in the Triassic, most mammals look the same.

They are small and furry and live in burrows in the underbrush, venturing out when it gets dark to hunt for tasty insects.

MORGANUCODON
(MOR-GAN-OOK-OH-DON)

They're hatching from eggs! What kind of mammal hatches from eggs?

For a long time, ALL mammals did. Some mammals still do, like platypuses and echidnas.

Dinosaurs are cool and huge. Bugs are small and boring. These are just the facts.

Small and boring? I take it you've never met a titanopteran (TIE-tan-OP-tur-un), then.

Probably because they won't survive past the end of the Triassic.

They're relatives of crickets, despite their resemblance to praying mantises.

The titanopteran uses its big spiky front legs to grab any insects, reptiles, and even mammals it feels like taking a bite out of.

Ooo, and here are some other very important insects!

34

Phylogenetic trees (FILE-oh-jen-ETT-ik) trees are used by scientists to map out the history of what organisms came from what other organisms.

YOU

NIECE

NEPHEW

SISTER

SISTER-IN-LAW

COUSIN

COUSIN

AUNT

DAD

UNCLE

MOM

GRANDPARENTS

They basically show how organisms evolved, how they're related, and how they're different. It's a lot like a family tree.

But instead of human families, we're going to talk about archosaurs!

We start by drawing a **node**.

ARCHOSAURS

This little dot is the common ancestor from which all archosaurs evolved.

From there, we draw "branches" to other nodes, which each represent one of the groups that evolved from that ancestor.

The groups that come from the same node are called **sister groups**, because they're kind of like siblings!

POSTOSUCHUS

CROCODYLOMORPHS

AETOSAURS

But how do we know when to split a group into sister groups?

The groups split when they develop different traits than those of their ancestors.

For example, let's draw this node and say it's the ancestor of pterosaurs and dinosaurs.

CROCODYLOMOPHS

Some of this ancestor's descendants evolved to have their legs directly beneath their body, not sprawled out.

This group is the dinosaurs.

WOWZA

CHECK ME OUT

Another group of descendants evolved wings and hollow bones, and this group is the pterosaurs.

But you said theropods also have hollow bones.

Ah, but these groups evolved hollow bones *after* they'd split apart.

Just because an organism evolves the same traits as another doesn't mean that organism has become the other!

HEY! QUIT BITIN' MY STYLE!

Now, within the group of dinosaurs, there are two main groups, which are defined by their different hips.

SO LONG, SUCKERS!!

ORNITHISCHIANS

DINOSAURS

PTEROSAURS

One of these is the **ornithischians** (OR-ni-THISK-ee-ans), like Stegosaurus and Triceratops and many others we'll be meeting soon.

Ornithischian means "bird-hipped" because their hip bones are pretty similar to a bird's hip bones.

THIS PART IN PARTICULAR

But birds actually belong to the other group of dinosaurs, the "lizard-hipped" **saurischians** (SAWR-ISH-ee-ans). That hip structure is another case of convergent evolution!

SAURISCHIANS

ORNITHISCHIANS

DINOSAUR

Saurischia contains two groups of dinosaurs we just met, the sauropods and the theropods.

I mentioned earlier that birds are dinosaurs. They are a kind of theropod.

NOT BIRDS

BIRDS

The theropod node can be divided into these two groups.

Birds and nonbird theropods are actually so similar...

NOT BIRDS

BIRDS

...it can be difficult to figure out when to call a dinosaur a bird!

WHAT IS THAT

So basically, birds are a type of dinosaur and dinosaurs are a type of archosaur...

NOOOOOO I'VE BEEN DETHRONED

... like how humans are a type of primate and primates are a type of mammal.

So does this make a little more sense now?

YEAH.

Heck yeah, phylogenetic trees are **awesome!**

38

...or not.

Aw, don't hurt little Compsognathus's (COMP-so-NATHE-uss) feelings. It is very special. It's one of the smallest non-avian dinosaurs!

Sure, it's not very intimidating (though it certainly is to the insects, mammals, and lizards of this region)...

...but it doesn't have to be big and scary to be important.

What does "non-avian" mean?

"Aves" is the group name for birds, and "avian" means of or relating to birds.

When we talk about all the dinosaurs that aren't birds, we call them **non-avian dinosaurs.**

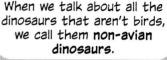

Though the line between avian and non-avian dinosaurs can be a little blurry.

Like with Archaeopteryx (AR-kee-OP-ter-iks).

It shares a lot of traits with birds, and is clearly at least closely related to the earliest birds.

But it also shares a lot of traits with non-avian theropods.

ARCHAEOPTERYX

BIRD

NON-AVIAN DINOSAUR

So paleontologists are always arguing about which group it belongs to!

But I thought birds evolved FROM dinosaurs. How could they evolve before the dinosaurs died out?

Birds ARE dinosaurs, AND they evolved from dinosaurs.

Just because something evolved from something else doesn't mean the original thing disappears.

AURORNIS, A BIRD

(OH-ROR-niss)

Like how there are both dogs and wolves, even though dogs evolved from wolves!

And eventually, they became honest-to-goodness feathers.

PEEP

You can actually see this whole process happening on a bird as it grows inside the egg!

But warmth wasn't the only reason feathers evolved to look the way they do.

AHEM

It was also an adaptation to attract the ladies.

In our time, many birds have very decorative, colorful feathers that they use to attract mates.

PEACOCK

BIRD OF PARADISE

And these mating displays are part of why feathers became so complicated!

LOOK AT ME

CONFUCIUSORNIS (KON-FEW-SHUS-OR-NISS)

So that's why non-avian dinosaurs sometimes have birdlike feathers? Because the feathers didn't evolve for flying, they evolved for display?

Right-o, excellent deduction!

But how did dinosaurs start flying in the first place?

Ah, that's something paleontologists are still arguing about.

They do that a lot, don't they?

Yes, but it's because there is still so much we don't know!

With each new generation of paleontologists, we learn even more about the world that existed before ours.

But currently, the most widely accepted theory is that dinosaurs used their wings to help them climb up trees faster.

They would flap their arms to help them jump farther up the trees.

Which helped them get away from predators as well as hunt.

(This is something the chicks of some birds do in our time!)

Eventually, the wings of some of these dinosaurs evolved to be much better at flapping...

...until they could fly.

Wow, getting up in the air takes a lot of steps!

Yeah, it's not exactly easy. But you know what IS easy...

Traveling through time and space!

THE EARLY-ISH, ALMOST-MIDDLE CRETACEOUS

Speaking of awesome creatures, there is a spectacular beast roaming the Laurasian plains.

It's Acrocanthosaurus (AK-ro-KANTH-oh-SAWR-uss), the largest land-dwelling theropod we've found. It can grow up to 38 feet long!

Though that's not to say the biggest is the best.

There are some smaller theropods in this region that are just as magnificent, and much more famous, such as Deinonychus (DINE-oh-NIKE-uss).

Deinonychus looks so familiar. It's like the Velociraptors on TV, but with feathers!

Yeah, due to some confusion with names back in the 1990s, a lot of people think Velociraptors are supposed to look like Deinonychus.

But they're wrong. This is Deinonychus, in all its feathery glory.

Wait, does that mean Velociraptors aren't real?

Oh no, they're real.

But they don't look like that. We'll meet some later, you'll see.

NORTHEASTERN LAURASIA THIS-A-WAY

Meanwhile, farther east in what will one day be Mongolia, theropods are filling some new and exciting niches.

There are now remarkable herbivorous theropods such as Alxasaurus (AL-ksa-SAWR-uss).

Alxasaurus has huge claws, which it uses to rip tasty leaves from branches.

These claws are also probably pretty handy in defending the herbivore against local predators, like this Xiongguanlong (shong-GWAN-long), another relative of Tyrannosaurus rex.

There are also some small theropods that make their home here, such as birds and Sinornithoides (sy-NOR-nith-OY-deez).

It's a member of one of the smartest groups of dinosaurs.

It's probably not as smart as, say, a crow, but it's still pretty smart!

Crows are smart...?

Yeah, kid! They remember faces. They can use *tools*.

Respect the crows.

Now let's see what's going on down among the crocodylomorphs of Gondwana...

Yay, crocs!!

CRUNCH

Several new groups of mammals have evolved at this point, including the three groups that exist in our time.

These groups each give birth and care for their babies in different ways.

The first group is the **placental** (pluh-SEN-tull) **mammals**, the group we belong to. They give birth to live young, unlike many vertebrates, which lay eggs.

Little Eomaia (EE-oh-MY-ah) here is our closest relative in this time period!

Eomaia shares these forests with Sinodelphys (SIN-oh-DELF-ees), the first of the **marsupials** (mar-SOOP-ee-als).

Marsupials give birth to live young, but they carry their babies in a pouch of skin on their stomachs until they're big enough to walk on their own.

You've probably heard about the marsupials that are around in our time, like kangaroos and koalas, and you may have seen one in your backyard: American opossums!

Meanwhile, down in the southeastern corner of Gondwana (in what will one day be Australia)...

...we find Steropodon (stare-OH-poh-don), the first **monotreme** (MON-oh-treem).

Monotremes lay eggs! Steropodon also has a bill, kind of like that of a duck, which is something the monotremes of our time also have.

Hold on, let me guess: Most of these mammals lived in trees or burrows and ate mostly insects?

AND seeds!

But yes, you're correct. All throughout the Mesozoic, mammals occupy this niche.

It works well for them, so they don't need to do much changing.

So um. About T. rex, though.

Not that I don't appreciate all this other stuff, but are we gonna, like...

...see one soon?

I guess it is about time for us to head off to our next stop, isn't it?

Let's head **44 million years forward,** to...

THE LATE CRETACEOUS

In our time, they help keep the local insect populations from becoming overcrowded.

They ensure that there is enough food and space for all the insects and other creatures to live comfortably.

OH NO, JIM!

OOOO MORE FOOD FOR ME THOUGH

Plus, if sawflies had died out back in the Triassic, we wouldn't have bees, either!

And without bees, flowers may never have become as widespread as they are.

And we wouldn't have the delicious fruits and vegetables that we love so much.

Okay... you're right.

Insects are pretty important, and even the ones that are scary probably fill necessary roles in the world.

Hooray! I knew you'd learn to love insects eventually.

Now let's get out of here. I may appreciate hymenopterans, but I don't appreciate being stung.

INTRUDER!!

INTRUDER! INTRUDER!!!

86

These sauropods have to defend themselves against the massive, menacing Carnotaurus (KAR-no-TOR-uss)!

Carnotaurus is a relative of the Kryptops we met back in the Early-ish Cretaceous, and you may notice they have some features in common.

Like their short faces and stubby little arms.

Wait, where's all its fluff? It's so naked.

And it has those bumpy things crocodylomorphs have. What are those?

Those bumpy things are called "scutes" (skyoots), small plates of bone under the skin.

AUSTRORAPTOR
(OSS-STRO-RAP-TOR)

Carnotaurus doesn't have a coat of protofeathers because it lives in a very dry, hot climate and didn't need them, so they gradually lost them.

Some mammals in our time have lost their fur for reasons like this, such as humans!

Speaking of humans, this desert weather is way too hot and dry for my delicate human body.

Let's see what the dinosaurs in a cooler climate are up to...

LAURASIA →

105

Wow.

COOL ANIMALS FROM OTHER TIMES

MICRORAPTOR
(MIKE-RO-RAP-TOR)
LIVED
130-125 MYA
(MILLION YEARS
AGO)

This is a non-avian dinosaur that had wings not only on its front limbs, but on its back limbs as well.

It wasn't a very good flier, but it could glide pretty well, using its leg wings to help steer while in the air.

UTAHRAPTOR
(YU-TAH-RAP-TOR)
LIVED 126 MYA

One of the largest dinosaurs in its group, which includes Deinonychus and Velociraptor.

KAPROSUCHUS
(KAP-RO-SOOK-uss)
LIVED 95 MYA

Nicknamed "the boar croc" because of its intense tusklike teeth. It was one of those crocs that ran around on land, and it is very cool, I think.

Its name means "pancake crocodile" because its face looks like a big flat pancake, if pancakes had teeth.

LAGANOSUCHUS
(LAG-AN-OH-SOOK-uss)
LIVED 95 MYA

ARCHELON
(ARK-ELL-ON)
LIVED 75 MYA

The largest sea turtle that has ever been found.

PACHYCEPHALOSAURS

CERATOPSIANS

IGUANODONTS

HADROSAURS

STEGOSAURS

ANKYLOSAURS

PTEROSAURS

ORNITHISCHIA

ORNITHODIRA

BIRDS

THEROPODA

SAURISCHIA

NOT BIRDS

SAUROPODS

MONOTREMES

MARSUPIALS

PLACENTAL MAMMALS

GLOSSARY

Amphibian: Cold-blooded animals whose eggs don't have thick shells and must be laid in water to keep from dehydrating.

Bird: A kind of dinosaur with a toothless beak and a short tail.

Carnivore: "Carn-" means meat and "-vore" means eat, so a carnivore is a creature that eats meat, such as Tyrannosaurus rex.

Cephalopod: A group of invertebrates that includes octopus, squid, cuttlefish, and nautilus.

Cold-blooded: Creatures that don't produce their own heat and rely on the sun for warmth.

Common ancestor: A creature that evolved into different groups of creatures. These groups have an ancestor in common.

Coniferous: Plants with needle-like leaves.

Convergent evolution: When multiple creatures evolve similar characteristics, despite not being related. For example, dolphins and sharks look very similar, even though one is a mammal and one is a fish.

Deciduous: Plants that shed their leaves as the seasons change.

Ecological niche: Where a creature lives, what it eats, and what eats it.

Evolution: When creatures develop new traits that help them survive and have babies.

Flowering plants: Plants that use flowers to transport their pollen to other plants.

Gondwana: A southern supercontinent containing Africa, India, South America, Australia, and Antarctica.

Herbivore: "Herb-" means plant and "-vore" means eat, so an herbivore is a creature that eats plants, such as Diplodocus.

Ice caps: The frozen areas around the North and South poles that stay frozen all year round.

Laurasia: A northern supercontinent containing Europe, North America, and Asia.

Mammal: Warm-blooded animals that produce milk for their offspring.

Mass extinction: An event in which a large percentage of life on Earth dies out.

Mesozoic: "Meso-" means middle, and "-zoic" means animals, so "Mesozoic" means "middle animals." It is the era in which non-avian dinosaurs lived and died, stretching from 252 million years ago to 66 million years ago.

Mutation: A change in the DNA of a creature that causes it to develop a new and different trait than its parents. Sometimes these mutations help the animal live long enough to have more babies than its non-mutated relatives, and the mutation spreads, which is how evolution happens.

Non-avian dinosaur: "Avian" means "of or relating to birds," so a non-avian dinosaur is any dinosaur that is not a bird.

Omnivore: "Omni-" means all, so an omnivore is a creature that eats both meat and plants, such as Anzu.

Paleontologist: A person who studies fossils.

Phylogenetic tree: A branching map showing what creatures evolved from what other creatures, and how they are all related. It's a lot like a family tree.

Protofeather: A hairlike fiber that eventually evolved into feathers. "Proto-" means first, so "protofeathers" means "first feathers."

Supercontinent: A very large landmass composed of several groups of continental plates, which are the large sheets of rock that float across the earth's surface.

Vertebrate: An animal with a backbone. The bones in your spine are called vertebrae, so an animal with a spine is called a vertebrate.

Warm-blooded: Creatures that produce their own heat, such as humans.

Abby Howard is a full-time cartoonist living in Boston with her cat and snake. She loves dinosaurs, pterosaurs, and all their extinct friends, and would go back in time in a heartbeat—even if it meant she was eaten or stepped on immediately.

What did Earth look like *before* the dinosaurs?

Find out in **Ocean Renegades!**

Turn the page for a bonus excerpt.

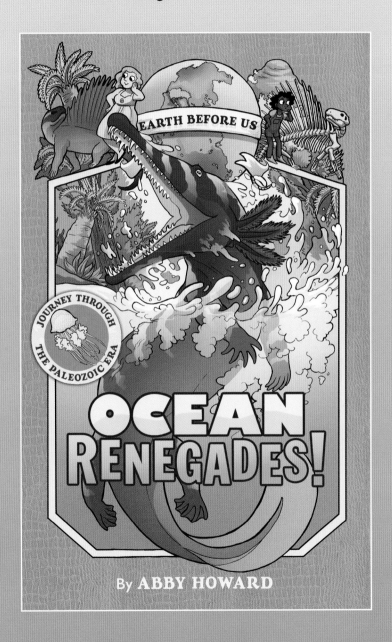

EARTH BEFORE US

JOURNEY THROUGH THE PALEOZOIC ERA

OCEAN RENEGADES!

By ABBY HOWARD

Bye, Mom and Dad!

Have fun on your business trip!

And thus begins our week of fun.

What do you want to do first, Ronnie?

Oh, you know...

Maybe further my education and see some cool animals?

Some cool *ancient* animals?

I know just the thing!

We'll go to my favorite place in the whole world...

Okay, I think we've seen all the fish now. Can we go?

We could still go check out those swings.

Anything but more jellyfish.

Are you not filled with amazement at every turn?

Do these creatures not overwhelm you with the beauty of the world?

Uh... I guess the lionfish looked pretty...

But many of these animals were floating and swimming through the oceans long before mammals evolved...

... long before the dinosaurs ruled the world...

... long before anything even set foot on land.

They are beautiful and ancient and wondrous.

They are true survivors, having lived through countless mass extinctions, changing and evolving to suit the constant fluctuations of the environment.

They should be cherished and honored by we humble mammals.

But they're booooring.

Though maybe it'd help me appreciate these fish and things...

...if I had more of a *hands-on* learning experience?

"Hands-on," you say?

They have a touch pool over there. We could go pet some horseshoe crabs!

No, no.

TOUCH POOL

I mean if we saw their long-dead and probably amazing ancestors.

They have a documentary on the evolution of fish.

There's a showing in ten minutes!

FISH
WHAT ARE THEY

PIZZA IN HD

NO!

I mean we should go back in time again and see some cool animals!

Ah, what an excellent suggestion!

Hmm...

Come along, young Ronnie!

We'll go back to the very origin of animals themselves.

We'll discover what the land was like...

...before the dinosaurs!

The things I do to see ancient beasts...

When we last went back in time, the farthest we traveled was 205 million years ago, to the late Triassic.

THE LEARNING CENTER

...right after we freshen up on evolution.

How about *you* teach *me* how it works this time?

Um...

Okay, so!

Evolution is what happens when a group of creatures changes over time and becomes...

...better...

Yes, Miss Lernin?

Better at what?

Better at all kinds of things! Sometimes the changes help them get food, sometimes they help the animals defend themselves, and sometimes they help them get dates.

PRETTY FEATHERS
CLAWS
LONG BEAK

Yes, Miss Lernin?

What are the changes called?

Mutations (mew-TAY-shuns)!

Mutations are changes to the DNA that sometimes help an animal survive longer and make more babies than other members of its species.

That means those mutations are passed on to the animal's babies, who pass it on to their babies, and so on and so on...

LONG BEAK MUTATION

CAN REACH MORE FOOD

...Until you have a whole new species!

HUMMINGBIRD

Excellent grasp of the concept, Ronnie!

Thank you.

Indeed we can.

Now can we go check out some cool extinct creatures?

COLLECT THEM ALL!

CHECK OUT THESE OTHER
GREAT GRAPHIC NOVELS!